Drinks & Bites

TRUEBLOOD

Drinks & Bites

*Gianna Sobol, Alan Ball,
and Benjamin Hayes*

**RECIPES BY
Dawn Yanagihara**

Recipe Photographs by Alex Farnum

CHRONICLE BOOKS
SAN FRANCISCO

www.hbo.com

Library of Congress Cataloging-in-Publication Data:
Sobol, Gianna.
True Blood drinks and bites / by Gianna Sobol, Alan Ball, and Benjamin Hayes ; recipes by Dawn Yanagihara ; recipe photography by Alex Farnum.
pages cm
Includes index.
ISBN 978-1-4521-1818-5 (alk. paper)
1. Fruit drinks. 2. Desserts. 3. True blood (Television program) I. Ball, Alan, 1957- II. Title.

TX740.5.S63 2013
641.87'5--dc23

2012036768

Manufactured in China

MIX
Paper from
responsible sources
FSC® C104723

Design by Public
Prop styling by Christine Wolheim
Food styling by Robyn Valarik

True Blood series photographs by Prashant Gupta, Doug Hyun, John P. Johnson, Lacey Terrell, and Jaime Trueblood

Special thanks to James Costos, Stacey Abiraj, Josh Goodstadt, Janis Fein, Cara Grabowski, Robin Eisgrau, and Tom Bozzelli.

10 9 8 7 6 5 4 3 2 1

Chronicle Books LLC
680 Second Street
San Francisco, CA 94107
www.chroniclebooks.com

"*It's all about casting off the empty shell of what's dead and embracing the mysteries of what is yet to come.*

WE ARE GONNA HAVE A WICKED GOOD TIME TONIGHT. I CAN JUST FEEL IT IN MY BONES."

—Maryann Forrester

FOR TEETOTALERS

||||||||||||||||||||||||||||||||||||||||||||||||||||||||||||||||||||||||||||||

by Jessica Hamby

Bill turned me at the ripe age of seventeen; before my human life had barely even begun. I'd never kissed a boy or gone on a real date. Never read a racy romance novel. Not a single alcoholic drink had touched my lips (well, 'cept for that time me 'n' Sally Burns stole some of her dad's strawberry-flavored wine coolers, but that doesn't really count). I was on the brink of doin' just about everything awesome I'd been waitin' my whole life to do—and then came Bill Compton.

But I ain't bitter, honest. Bein' turned into a vampire was the best thing that ever happened to me. Hell, it was the only thing that ever happened to me. And shortly after, I kissed a boy, I went on that date, I devoured every book my parents' church banned. I did all the things normal teenagers do. But I never did get that drink. And you know what? I'm okay with it. There's all sortsa ways to enjoy a good cocktail without the booze. Especially if you're a vampire. My favorite (other than fresh from the source) is O neg with a twist of B pos. What about you?

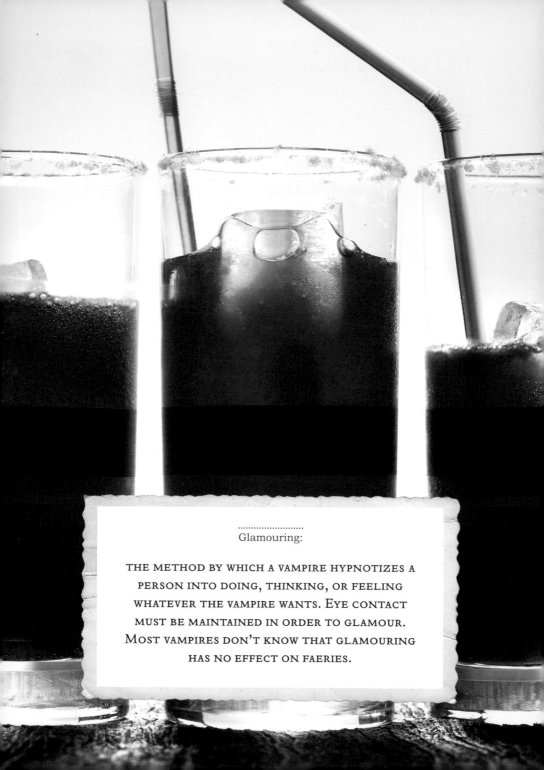

....
Glamouring:

THE METHOD BY WHICH A VAMPIRE HYPNOTIZES A
PERSON INTO DOING, THINKING, OR FEELING
WHATEVER THE VAMPIRE WANTS. EYE CONTACT
MUST BE MAINTAINED IN ORDER TO GLAMOUR.
MOST VAMPIRES DON'T KNOW THAT GLAMOURING
HAS NO EFFECT ON FAERIES.

Glamourade

◇◇◇◇◇◇◇◇◇◇◇◇◇◇◇◇◇◇◇◇◇◇◇◇◇◇◇◇◇◇

1¼ CUPS SUGAR, PLUS
3 TABLESPOONS

2½ CUPS (*10 ounces*) FROZEN
UNSWEETENED BLACKBERRIES

¼ CUP WATER

1 CUP FRESH LIME JUICE
(*about 5 limes*)

1 LIME WEDGE

ICE CUBES

ONE 1-LITER BOTTLE CHILLED
SPARKLING WATER

◇◇◇◇◇◇◇◇◇◇◇◇◇◇◇◇◇◇◇◇◇◇◇◇◇◇◇◇◇◇

In a medium saucepan, combine the 1¼ cups sugar, berries, and water. Bring the mixture to a gentle simmer over medium heat, stirring to dissolve the sugar. When the berries have just begun to soften and release some juice, remove the pan from the heat and set it aside for 10 minutes or so, until the berries are soft and squishy.

Using a rubber spatula, mash the berries to break them down a bit, and then transfer to a fine-mesh strainer set over a small bowl. Work the mixture with the spatula to force it through; really press down on it to extract as much juice as you can and scrape the bottom of the strainer a couple of times. Discard the goop that's left in the strainer. Let the purée cool to room temperature, about 10 minutes, and then transfer it to a pitcher. Stir in the lime juice.

When you're ready to glamour your guests, put the 3 tablespoons sugar in a small, wide dish or container. Working one at time, rub the rim of the drinking glasses with the cut edge of the lime wedge to moisten, and then invert each glass into the sugar to coat the rim. Fill the glasses with ice.

Gently pour the sparkling water into the pitcher and stir ever so gently to combine. Pour the Glamourade into the glasses and serve right away, making eye contact with your guests and telling them that they'd love to help you do the dishes postparty.

"FIGHTING CRIME—*it's a hell of a workout.*"

—Andy Bellefleur

SHERIFF ANDY BELLEFLEUR

Crime Quencher

◇◇◇◇◇◇◇◇◇◇◇◇◇◇◇◇◇◇◇◇◇◇◇◇◇◇◇◇◇◇◇◇◇◇◇

ABOUT 6 CUPS SEEDLESS WATERMELON CHUNKS CHILLED, PLUS THIN SLIVERS OF WATERMELON WITH RIND FOR GARNISH (optional)

1½ CUPS HULLED FRESH STRAWBERRIES, OR FROZEN UNSWEETENED STRAWBERRIES, THAWED

1½ TABLESPOONS FRESH LIME JUICE

2 TABLESPOONS SUGAR

PINCH OF SALT

2 CUPS CHILLED SPARKLING WATER

ICE CUBES

◇◇◇◇◇◇◇◇◇◇◇◇◇◇◇◇◇◇◇◇◇◇◇◇◇◇◇◇◇◇◇◇◇◇◇

MAKES ABOUT 6 CUPS,
SERVES 6 TO 8

Pile the melon chunks and berries into a blender; add the lime juice, sugar, and salt; and purée until smooth. Or, if you're bothered by any seeds and/or any chunks that didn't break down, pour the purée into a fine-mesh strainer set over a large bowl and work the mixture with a rubber spatula to force it through; really press down on it to extract as much juice as you can. Discard the stuff that's left in the strainer. Pour the purée into a large pitcher. Cover and refrigerate until nice and chilled, at least 1 hour.

When you're ready for some quenching, gently pour the sparkling water into the pitcher and stir ever so lightly to combine. Fill drinking glasses with ice and pour in the liquid. Garnish each glass with a watermelon sliver, if desired, and serve right away.

"I JUST REDECORATED THE GUEST ROOM.
Wait 'til you see the bed, Bill. It's marvelous.
IT ONCE BELONGED TO COUNTESS
ELIZABETH BÁTHORY, HUNGARY'S
LEGENDARY SERIAL KILLER.
*Rumor has it that she loved to torture
virgins and bathe in their blood.*"

—Talbot

Virgin Blood

ICE CUBES

½ OUNCE GOOD-QUALITY GRENADINE

1 OUNCE FRESH GRAPEFRUIT JUICE

2 OUNCES CHILLED TART CHERRY JUICE

2 OUNCES CHILLED GINGER ALE

2 OR 3 MARASCHINO CHERRIES FOR GARNISH

Fill a double old-fashioned glass with ice. Pour in the grenadine, grapefruit juice, cherry juice, and ginger ale. Stir gently to combine.

Doll up the drink by skewering the maraschino cherries on a cocktail pick and lay the pick across the rim of the glass. Serve right away.

Lilith: *According to vampire religion, Lilith was the first earthbound vampire.* The Vampire Bible, which predates the Old Testament, explains that God created Lilith in His own image, and subsequently created Adam and Eve to be Her food.

Blood of Lilith

3 CUPS FROZEN MIXED UNSWEETENED BERRIES, PLUS MORE FOR GARNISH *(optional)*

2 TABLESPOONS SUGAR

¼ CUP WATER

1 TABLESPOON FRESH LEMON JUICE

2½ CUPS CRANBERRY JUICE COCKTAIL

2½ CUPS CHILLED ORANGINA

ICE CUBES

In a medium saucepan, combine the berries, sugar, and water. Bring the mixture to a gentle simmer over medium heat, stirring to dissolve the sugar. When the berries have just begun to soften and release some juice, remove the pan from the heat and set it aside for about 10 minutes, or until the berries are soft and squishy.

Transfer the berry mixture to a blender, purée until smooth, and then pour the purée into a large fine-mesh strainer set over a bowl. Work the mixture with the spatula to force it through; really press down on it to extract as much juice as you can and scrape the bottom of the strainer a couple of times. Discard the goop that's left in the strainer. Let the purée cool to room temperature, about 10 minutes, and then pour it into a large pitcher. Stir in the lemon juice and cranberry juice cocktail and refrigerate until chilled.

When you're ready to pass some plasma, gently pour in the chilled Orangina and stir ever so lightly. Fill drinking glasses with ice and pour in the punch. If desired, drop in a few berries as a garnish and serve right away.

Lumière Sparklers

⅓ CUP WATER

⅓ CUP SUGAR

6 TO 8 SLICES PEELED FRESH
GINGER, ⅛ INCH THICK, CRUSHED

1 TABLESPOON FRESH ROSEMARY
LEAVES, COARSELY CHOPPED,
PLUS 6 SMALL SPRIGS FOR GARNISH

6 TABLESPOONS CHILLED
UNSWEETENED POMEGRANATE
JUICE

ONE 750-MILLILITER BOTTLE
CHILLED SPARKLING APPLE CIDER

In a small saucepan, bring the water, sugar, and ginger to a boil over medium heat, stirring occasionally to help the sugar dissolve. Add the chopped rosemary and swirl the pan. Turn off the heat, cover, and let the flavors infuse for 30 minutes.

Pour the infused sugar syrup through a fine-mesh strainer into a small bowl. Cover and refrigerate until chilled, at least 30 minutes. Throw out the stuff in the strainer.

When you're ready to serve, measure a scant 1 tablespoon of sugar syrup into each of six chilled champagne flutes or cocktail glasses, followed by 1 tablespoon of pomegranate juice. Pour ½ cup of sparkling cider into each glass. Drop a rosemary sprig into each drink and serve right away.

MAKES 6 DRINKS

"I knew it was
faeries, 'cause they
blew me and
*Andy out of there with
light bombs from
their hands.*"

—Jason Stackhouse

Wiccan Brew

2 CINNAMON STICKS

8 ALLSPICE BERRIES

½ TEASPOON BLACK PEPPERCORNS

1 SMALL DRIED RED CHILE (*optional*)

3 STRIPS ORANGE ZEST (*removed with a vegetable peeler*)

2 SLICES PEELED FRESH GINGER, ¼ INCH THICK, CRUSHED

4 CUPS APPLE CIDER

2 CUPS UNSWEETENED POMEGRANATE JUICE

3 TABLESPOONS LIGHT OR DARK BROWN SUGAR

POMEGRANATE SEEDS FOR GARNISH (*optional*)

Bundle the cinnamon sticks, allspice berries, peppercorns, dried chile, orange zest, and ginger in a doubled-up piece of cheesecloth and secure with a length of kitchen twine.

In a large nonreactive saucepan or cauldron, combine the apple cider, pomegranate juice, brown sugar, and spice bundle and bring to a simmer over medium-high heat. Cover the pan, reduce the heat to low, and let the mixture bubble gently until the liquid is fragrant and infused, about 45 minutes.

Remove and discard the spice bundle. Ladle the brew into heat-proof mugs and garnish with pomegranate seeds, if desired. Serve right away.

> *"There ain't no spell
> that can't be
> undone if you got the juice."*
>
> — Holly Cleary

"Your hair is like a sunset after a bomb went off. **PRETTY!**"

—Terry Bellefleur

Redhead Refresher

◇◇◇◇◇◇◇◇◇◇◇◇◇◇◇◇◇◇◇◇◇◇◇◇◇◇◇◇◇◇◇◇

6 CUPS WATER

½ CUP DRIED HIBISCUS FLOWERS
(*also called flor de Jamaica*)

½ CUP FRESH MINT LEAVES, TORN, PLUS
FRESH MINT SPRIGS FOR GARNISH

¼ CUP PLUS 2 TABLESPOONS SUGAR

ICE CUBES

MAKES ABOUT 6 CUPS,
SERVES 6 TO 8

◇◇◇◇◇◇◇◇◇◇◇◇◇◇◇◇◇◇◇◇◇◇◇◇◇◇◇◇◇◇◇◇◇◇◇◇

In a small saucepan, bring 3 cups of the water to a rolling boil over high heat. Add the hibiscus and mint leaves, and then shut off the heat. Give the mixture a stir, cover the pan, and set a timer for 20 minutes.

When the timer goes off, pour the mixture through a fine-mesh strainer into a heat-proof pitcher. Dump out all that scary-looking junk in the strainer. Add the sugar to the pitcher and stir until it dissolves. Pour in 3 cups of cool water to bring down the temperature, cover the pitcher, and refrigerate until nice and chilled, at least 1 hour.

Fill drinking glasses with ice, and then pour in the refresher. Garnish each glass with a mint sprig and serve right away.

Teatime in Bon Temps

10 BLACK TEA BAGS

8 CUPS PLUS 2 TABLESPOONS WATER

¼ CUP SUGAR

2½ CUPS FROZEN UNSWEETENED
PEELED PEACH SLICES, THAWED,
PLUS MORE FOR GARNISH

½ CUP FROZEN UNSWEETENED
RASPBERRIES, THAWED, PLUS MORE
FOR GARNISH

ICE CUBES

Toss the tea bags into a large heat-proof pitcher.

In a small saucepan or teakettle, bring 4 cups of the water to a rolling boil. Pour the boiling water into the pitcher and steep the tea for 5 minutes.

Remove the tea bags (don't wring them dry or the tea will be bitter) and discard. Add the sugar to the pitcher and stir until it dissolves. Pour in 4 cups of cool water to bring down the temperature and set the pitcher aside.

In a blender, purée the 2½ cups peaches and ½ cup raspberries with the remaining 2 tablespoons water until smooth. Transfer the purée to a fine-mesh strainer set over a medium bowl and work the mixture with a rubber spatula to force it through. Discard the junk that's left in the strainer.

When the tea has cooled to room temperature, stir in the fruit purée. Refrigerate until nice and cold, at least 1 hour.

When you're ready to serve, fill drinking glasses with ice. Stir the tea to recombine and pour it into the glasses. Garnish with peach slices and/or raspberries and serve right away.

Andy and Terry's grandmother, Caroline, used to throw the most decadent tea parties for the society ladies of Bon Temps in the garden of the Bellefleur mansion.
But when people caught on to the fact that she was slipping whiskey into her tea and getting sloshed, attendance dwindled, and eventually she stopped hosting teatime altogether.

FOR BOOZEHOUNDS

||||||||||||||||||||||||||||||||||||||||||||||||||||||||||||||||||||||

by Pam Swynford De Beaufort

If you think the only thing I'm good for is a snarky comeback and killer heels, then drop by Fangtasia any night of the week. I throw a damn good party. Eric and I have been at the helm of one of Louisiana's most successful vampire bars since the Great Revelation, and something tells me it's not on account of Eric's "hosting" skills. Quite frankly, he's more of the business guy. The crowd? The cocktails? The ambience? That's me.

When running a bar, it's of the utmost importance to know your clientele. And while it's no secret the vampires are here for the humans and the humans are here for the vampires, why rush through the foreplay? People need a little warming up, a little lubrication, before they can admit to themselves that they really just want to have some vampire fun. And, hey, whatever works, right?

Now, being a vampire, I may not be able to enjoy the kind of pleasure a well-mixed cocktail brings, but I sure know how to give pleasure. I make some of the best drinks you'll experience in your short, pathetic human lives. Take a look.

Screwed Driver

ICE CUBES

1½ OUNCES CACHAÇA

½ OUNCE TRIPLE SEC

2 DASHES ORANGE BITTERS

4 OUNCES BLOOD ORANGE JUICE

1 FRESH MINT SPRIG

Fill a highball glass with ice. Pour in the cachaça, triple sec, orange bitters, and blood orange juice. Stir well. Smack the mint sprig between the palms of your hands to release its fragrance, and then garnish the cocktail. Serve right away.

"I AM AN EXCELLENT DRIVER.
But you cannot prepare for a naked lady and a hog in the middle of the road!"

—Tara Thornton

"There is a REASON you find vampires irresistible, A REASON YOU SLUT YOUR HEART OUT TO EVERY CUTE GUY OUT THERE WITH A PAIR OF FANGS."

—The Elder

Faerie Blood

1½ TO 2 TABLESPOONS SUGAR

1 LEMON WEDGE

1 OUNCE ST-GERMAIN ELDERFLOWER LIQUEUR

2 TEASPOONS CAMPARI

½ TEASPOON FRESH LEMON JUICE

3 OUNCES CHILLED SPARKLING ROSÉ WINE

Put the sugar in a ramekin. Rub the rim of a champagne flute with the cut side of the lemon wedge to moisten, and then invert the glass into the sugar to coat the rim. If you have the time, refrigerate the glass to chill it and allow the sugar to harden, about 10 minutes.

Pour the St-Germain, Campari, and lemon juice into the glass. Top with the sparkling wine and serve right away.

Sex Is a Bitch

ICE CUBES

1½ OUNCES VODKA

½ OUNCE CAMPARI

½ OUNCE SWEET VERMOUTH

2 OUNCES CRANBERRY JUICE
COCKTAIL

1½ OUNCES FRESH
GRAPEFRUIT JUICE

1 QUARTER-MOON
GRAPEFRUIT SLICE

Fill a double old-fashioned glass with ice. Pour in the vodka, Campari, vermouth, cranberry juice cocktail, and grapefruit juice. Stir well. Garnish with the grapefruit slice and serve right away.

MAKES 1 DRINK

"I swear, as much as I love it, **EVERY BAD THING THAT'S EVER HAPPENED TO ME IS 'CAUSE OF SEX."**

—Jason Stackhouse

Lou Pine's Special

ICE CUBES

2 OUNCES GOSLING'S BLACK
SEAL RUM

1 OUNCE BLOOD ORANGE JUICE

½ OUNCE MOONSHINE
(*white dog whiskey*)

6 OUNCES GINGER BEER
(*not ginger ale!*)

1 LIME WEDGE

Fill a highball glass with ice. Pour in the rum, blood
orange juice, moonshine, and ginger beer. Garnish with
the lime wedge. Serve right away.

MAKES 1 DRINK

LOU PINE'S IS A PUN ON THE WORD *LUPINE*, WHICH
REFERS TO SOMETHING HAVING CHARACTERISTICS OF
A WOLF. THE BAR WAS ORIGINALLY OPENED IN THE
LATE '70S BY A ROGUE PACK OF WOLVES THAT WAS
LOOKING TO SETTLE DOWN, AND HAS SINCE BECOME
A FAVORITE OF PACKS BOTH LOCAL AND FROM AFAR.
THE BAR'S BOUNCER, HOLLIS, ALWAYS SAYS, "LOU
PINE'S HAS BOOZE, BITCHES, AND BROTHERHOOD.
WHAT MORE COULD A WOLF NEED?"

Bloody Sundress

1½ OUNCES VODKA

1 OUNCE LIMONCELLO

1 OUNCE UNSWEETENED POMEGRANATE JUICE

½ OUNCE FRESH LIME JUICE

½ TEASPOON SIMPLE SYRUP (*recipe follows*)

3 OR 4 DROPS ROSEWATER

ICE CUBES

1 LEMON TWIST

Put a cocktail glass in the freezer to chill.

Pour the vodka, limoncello, pomegranate juice, lime juice, simple syrup, and rosewater into a cocktail shaker and drop in some ice. Shake until well chilled, remove the glass from the freezer, and strain the cocktail into the chilled glass. Garnish with the lemon twist and serve right away.

Simple Syrup

1 CUP SUGAR

1 CUP WATER

In a small saucepan over medium heat, combine the sugar and water. Heat the mixture, stirring, until the sugar dissolves. Pour the syrup into a clean jar or bottle with a tight-fitting lid and let cool before using. Simple syrup will keep, tightly sealed and refrigerated, for a vamp's age.

"Do not tell me you'd put our entire species at risk for a gash in a sundress."

—Pam Swynford De Beaufort

Stake House Special

4 OR 5 SWEET RED CHERRIES, PITTED

¼ OUNCE SIMPLE SYRUP (*page 42*)

1½ OUNCES MOONSHINE (*white dog whiskey*)

1½ TEASPOONS FRESH LEMON JUICE

ABOUT 5 ICE CUBES

1 LEMON TWIST

MAKES 1 DRINK

Combine the cherries and simple syrup in a mixing glass and muddle until the cherries are juicy and broken down into bits. Add the moonshine, lemon juice, and ice cubes. Shake well, and then pour, unstrained, into an old-fashioned glass. Garnish with the lemon twist and serve right away.

THE STAKE HOUSE IS BON TEMPS' LOCAL ANTI-
VAMPIRE HOME PROTECTION STORE. IT OPENED IN
THE AFTERMATH OF THE RUSSELL EDGINGTON
SCANDAL, CATERING TO HUMANS LOOKING TO ARM
THEMSELVES AGAINST VAMPIRES OR ANY OTHER
SUPERNATURAL BEINGS. THE STAKE HOUSE SELLS
STAKES, COLLOIDAL SILVER MISTERS, CROSSBOWS,
WOODEN BULLETS, ETC.

"You can't buy your way
out of everything."

—Talbot

"OF COURSE I CAN!
This is America."

—Russell Edgington

Undead Millionaire

¾ OUNCE COGNAC

¼ OUNCE GRAND MARNIER

1½ OUNCES RED LILLET

4 OR 5 DASHES ORANGE BITTERS

1 DROP VANILLA EXTRACT

ICE CUBES

1 THIN ORANGE SLICE

Put a cocktail glass in the freezer to chill.

Pour the cognac, Grand Marnier, Lillet, orange bitters, and vanilla into a cocktail shaker and drop in some ice. Shake until well chilled, and then strain into the chilled glass. Garnish with the orange slice and serve right away.

Spirit Lifter

MAKES 1 DRINK

ICE CUBES

1½ OUNCES SOUTHERN COMFORT

1 OUNCE MOONSHINE (*white dog whiskey*)

½ OUNCE FRESH LEMON JUICE

1 TEASPOON GRENADINE

3 OUNCES COCA-COLA

Fill a highball glass with ice. Pour in the Southern Comfort, moonshine, lemon juice, and grenadine. Top off with the Coca-Cola and stir gently. Serve right away.

> "*Never really thought I was smart enough to get depressed,* BUT HERE I AM."
>
> —Jason Stackhouse

MoonGoddess

1 OUNCE GIN

1 OUNCE GREEN CHARTREUSE

1 OUNCE FRESH LIME JUICE

¼ OUNCE SIMPLE SYRUP
(*page 42*)

ICE CUBES

1 CANTALOUPE WEDGE

Put a cocktail glass in the freezer to chill.

Pour the gin, Chartreuse, lime juice, and simple syrup into a mixing glass and drop in some ice. Stir until well chilled, and then strain into the chilled glass. Skewer the cantaloupe on a cocktail pick, garnish, and serve right away.

MOONGODDESS EMPORIUM WAS FIRST OPENED BY MARNIE STONEBROOK AND HER DEAR FRIEND AND MENTOR ALMA OLIVETTI IN 1995.

WHEN ALMA PASSED AWAY, FULL OWNERSHIP OF THE SHOP WAS LEFT IN MARNIE'S HANDS. SHORTLY THEREAFTER, MARNIE BEGAN HER INFAMOUS WICCAN CIRCLE.

True Death

MAKES 1 DRINK

1 LIME WEDGE

1½ OUNCES SILVER TEQUILA

3½ OUNCES FRESH ORANGE JUICE

ICE CUBES

1 TEASPOON GRENADINE

1 TEASPOON CRÈME DE CASSIS

Put a cocktail glass in the freezer to chill.

Squeeze the juice from the lime wedge into a cocktail shaker, and then pour in the tequila and orange juice. Add ice and shake until well chilled. Strain into the chilled glass. Spoon the grenadine down the side of the glass and let it sink to the bottom. Do the same with the crème de cassis. Serve right away.

> **"TELL HER I WAS BORN THE SAME NIGHT SHE FOUND ME.**
> *And because of her, I went to my True Death knowing what it means to love."*
>
> —Eric Northman

Bon Temps Sazerac

1 TEASPOON PERNOD

1 TEASPOON MAPLE SYRUP

4 DASHES PEYCHAUD'S BITTERS

2½ OUNCES BOURBON

ICE

1 LEMON TWIST

Pour the Pernod into a double old-fashioned glass and tilt the glass to coat the sides. Pour out the Pernod and put the glass in the freezer to chill.

Combine the maple syrup, bitters, and bourbon in a mixing glass and give the glass a couple of swirls to blend in the maple syrup. Add ice and stir until well chilled. Strain into the chilled glass, garnish with the lemon twist, and *laissez les bon temps rouler!*

MAKES 1 DRINK

BON TEMPS IS FRENCH FOR "GOOD TIMES."
THE TOWN IS LOCATED WITHIN RENARD PARISH, IN
THE NORTHERN REGION OF LOUISIANA, ABOUT
HALFWAY BETWEEN SHREVEPORT AND MONROE.
BON TEMPS BOASTS A POPULATION OF 2,712.

"GIVES IT A PUNGENT HINT OF MADNESS, A LITTLE TOUCH OF TOTAL ABANDON—*and I can tell that you are no stranger to total abandon.*"

—Maryann Forrester

Maenad à Trois

1 OUNCE DOMAINE DE
CANTON GINGER LIQUEUR

1 OUNCE PEACH PURÉE
(*recipe follows*)

3 OUNCES CHILLED PROSECCO

1 FROZEN PEACH SLICE
(*optional*)

Put a champagne flute in the freezer to chill.

Combine the ginger liqueur and peach purée in a mixing glass and stir. Add the Prosecco and stir gently to reduce the bubbliness. Pour the mixture into the chilled flute. Drop in the frozen peach slice, if desired, and serve right away.

Peach Purée

MAKES ABOUT 1 CUP, ENOUGH
TO MAKE 8 COCKTAILS

2 CUPS FROZEN
UNSWEETENED PEELED
PEACH SLICES, THAWED

2 TABLESPOONS WATER

In a blender, purée the peach slices with the water until smooth. Transfer to a small bowl, cover, and refrigerate until cold. The purée keeps for up to 3 days in a tightly sealed container in the refrigerator.

V Shooters

2 CUPS FROZEN MIXED UNSWEETENED BERRIES, THAWED

2 TABLESPOONS SUGAR

2 TABLESPOONS CRANBERRY JUICE COCKTAIL

1 TABLESPOON TRIPLE SEC

¼ CUP SOUTHERN COMFORT

Put the berries and sugar in a medium bowl and mash the hell out of the mixture with a potato masher. When the berries are reduced to a juicy pulp, transfer the mixture to a fine-mesh strainer set over a 2-cup measuring cup and work the mixture with a rubber spatula; really press down on it to extract as much juice as you can, and scrape the bottom of the strainer a couple of times. Discard the junk that's left in the strainer.

Add the cranberry juice cocktail and triple sec to the berry purée and stir well. Cover and refrigerate until cold. Put eight to ten shot glasses or similarly sized food-safe test tubes in the freezer or refrigerator to chill.

When the need for V strikes, add the Southern Comfort to the chilled berry mixture and stir well. Pour 1 to 1½ ounces (2 to 2½ tablespoons) into each shot glass and serve right away, but discreetly, of course.

"JESUS, TITS, AND GOD AMERICA, JASON.
What the f*** is happenin' to me?
I'm only good on the V, dude.
It's the only time I ever feel like I'm not
watchin' myself not livin' up to people's
expectations, and hatin' those people for
havin' expectations, and thinkin' about
hittin' them in the head with a bat."

—Andy Bellefleur

Sanguinista

½ ORANGE, THINLY SLICED

½ LEMON, THINLY SLICED

¼ CUP SUGAR

ONE 750-MILLILITER BOTTLE RED WINE

½ CUP FRESH ORANGE JUICE

¼ CUP COINTREAU OR GRAND MARNIER

ABOUT 2 CUPS ICE CUBES

Drop the orange and lemon slices into a large pitcher, add the sugar, and stir well. Let stand until the fruit begins to release some juice and the sugar begins to dissolve, about 20 minutes.

Pour in the wine, orange juice, and Cointreau and stir well. Cover the pitcher and refrigerate for at least 2 hours or up to 12 hours to let the flavors blend.

About 10 minutes before imbibing, add the ice and let stand for a few minutes to get the Sanguinista nice and cold. Pour into glasses and serve.

Sanguinist Movement:

A VAMPIRE POLITICAL FACTION WHOSE CORE BELIEF IS THAT HUMANS ARE AN INFERIOR SPECIES TO VAMPIRES AND SHOULD BE SUBJUGATED AND USED AS FOOD. BY DEFINITION, SANGUINISTAS ARE DEVOUT FOLLOWERS OF LILITH AND THE VAMPIRE BIBLE.

Tequila Brujo

2½ CUPS FROZEN UNSWEETENED STRAWBERRIES, THAWED

¼ CUP AGAVE SYRUP

3 TABLESPOONS GOOD-QUALITY GRENADINE (*or 2 tablespoons of the average stuff*)

1 CUP FRESH LIME JUICE

1 CUP SILVER TEQUILA

1 CUP COINTREAU OR TRIPLE SEC

ICE CUBES

2 TABLESPOONS SUGAR

1½ TEASPOONS KOSHER SALT

¼ TEASPOON CAYENNE PEPPER

1 LIME WEDGE

Combine the strawberries, agave syrup, and grenadine in a medium bowl and mash the hell out of the mixture with a potato masher. When the berries are reduced to a juicy pulp, transfer them to a large fine-mesh strainer set over a bowl and work the mixture with a rubber spatula; really press down on it to extract as much juice as you can and scrape the bottom of the strainer a couple of times. Discard the mess that's left in the strainer.

Pour the strawberry mixture into a large pitcher and add the lime juice, tequila, and Cointreau. Stir well, add about 2 cups of ice, and let stand (in the refrigerator, if you've got the room) for about 15 minutes to let the mixture get nice and cold.

Meanwhile, stir together the sugar, salt, and cayenne in a small, wide dish or container. Working one at time, rub the rims of six to eight double-old fashioned glasses with the cut edge of the lime wedge to moisten, and then invert each glass into the sugar mixture to coat the rim. Fill the glasses with ice.

Stir the Tequila Brujo to recombine, fill the glasses, and serve. ¡Ándale!

> "*I'm a* **brujo.** *A witch.*"
> —Jesus Velasquez

> "*You're a witch.* **You're a witch who's a nurse, who's a dude.**"
> —Lafayette Reynolds

"OH, THAT'S THE THING ABOUT BEIN' WITH VAMPS, AIN'T IT? YOU ALWAYS FORGET TO EAT. *I've lost thirty-seven pounds since I got this job. Way better than a fat farm!*"

—Ginger

Screaming Ginger

2 CUPS PINEAPPLE JUICE, PREFERABLY *not* FROM CONCENTRATE

2 CUPS FRESH ORANGE JUICE

2 CUPS DARK RUM

¼ CUP TRIPLE SEC

3 TABLESPOONS FRESH LIME JUICE

2 TABLESPOONS GRENADINE

ABOUT 3 TABLESPOONS GRATED PEELED FRESH GINGER

ICE CUBES

ONE 12-OUNCE CAN CHILLED CLUB SODA

ORANGE SLICES OR PINEAPPLE WEDGES FOR GARNISH

In a pitcher, combine the pineapple juice, orange juice, rum, triple sec, lime juice, and grenadine.

Put the grated ginger in a fine-mesh strainer set over a small bowl. With a soupspoon or rubber spatula, press down firmly on the ginger to extract the juice. Measure out 1 tablespoon of ginger juice and add it to the pitcher. (Dump out the fibers left in the strainer.) Cover and refrigerate until nice and cold, at least 1 hour.

When you're ready to serve, add about 1 cup of ice and the club soda to the pitcher and stir gently. Fill glasses with ice and pour in the punch. Garnish with fruit and serve right away.

"The blood,
drained of oxygen,
it's pure and thick—
you don't even have to try.
Her heart's pulsing.
Let it flow to you.
HER LIFE, IT'S YOURS. DRINK.
THIS IS WHO YOU ARE NOW. THE
TOP OF THE CHAIN. NO HUMAN
CAN HURT YOU ANY LONGER."

—Pam Swynford
De Beaufort

No Pain, No Drain

4 CUPS TOMATO JUICE

1½ CUPS VODKA

¼ CUP PLUS 2 TABLESPOONS
FRESH LEMON JUICE

2 TABLESPOONS PREPARED
HORSERADISH

1½ TABLESPOONS
WORCESTERSHIRE SAUCE

1 TABLESPOON BRINE FROM
PICKLED JALAPEÑOS OR
PICKLED OKRA

¼ TEASPOON FRESHLY
GROUND BLACK PEPPER

½ TEASPOON PAPRIKA

½ TEASPOON TABASCO SAUCE

¼ TEASPOON CELERY SALT

PICKLED COCKTAIL ONIONS

PICKLED JALAPEÑO SLICES OR
PICKLED OKRA

LEMON WEDGES

ICE CUBES

In a pitcher, stir together the tomato juice, vodka, lemon juice, horseradish, Worcestershire sauce, brine, pepper, paprika, Tabasco, and celery salt. Cover and refrigerate to allow the flavors to blend and the mixture to chill, at least 1 hour.

When you're ready to serve, skewer a cocktail onion, jalapeño slice, and lemon wedge on each of six to eight cocktail picks. Fill double old-fashioned glasses with ice. Stir the pitcher's contents to recombine and pour into the glasses. Garnish with the skewers and serve right away.

MAKES 6 CUPS,
SERVES 6 TO 8

BITES

||||||||||||||||||||||

by Maxine Fortenberry

The secret to bein' a good cook? Gettin' older.
The best dishes take oodles of practice, years of messin'
around with ingredients and tryin' new things. No
twenty-five-year-old hotshot is gonna whip up biscuits
better'n mine. Not even that cutie-pie Summer,
the gal Hoyt *shoulda* married.

Now, I know me 'n' Hoyt have our issues, but one thing
we agree on is that I make the best dang food in Renard
Parish. He likes to go over to Merlotte's for a burger and
fries sometimes to be sociable, but when he's real hungry,
he comes home to Mama. Because let's be honest, Mama
cooks best. So take a look at these recipes. Give 'em a try—
and then give 'em another try. Because like most things,
they get better with age.

Spiced Nuts

¼ CUP SUGAR

2 TEASPOONS KOSHER SALT

1½ TEASPOONS GROUND CINNAMON

1 TEASPOON CHILI POWDER

½ TEASPOON FRESHLY GROUND BLACK PEPPER

½ TEASPOON CAYENNE PEPPER

¼ TEASPOON GROUND ALLSPICE

1 EGG WHITE

¼ TEASPOON TABASCO SAUCE

2 CUPS RAW PECAN HALVES

1 CUP RAW WALNUT HALVES

1 CUP RAW CASHEWS

Preheat the oven to 325°F. Line a large rimmed baking sheet with parchment paper.

In a small bowl, stir together the sugar, salt, and spices until combined.

In a large bowl, whisk the egg white and Tabasco vigorously until the white is stiff enough to form soft mounds. Add the nuts and toss with a rubber spatula until evenly moistened. Pour in the sugar mixture and continue to toss and stir until the nuts are coated with sugar and spices.

Pour the nuts onto the prepared baking sheet, spread them out, and bake, stirring two or three times, until browned and fragrant, about 45 minutes. Let cool on the baking sheet on a wire rack; the nuts will crisp up with cooling. Break up any stuck-together pieces. Serve the nuts, or squirrel them away in an airtight container for up to 2 weeks.

> "SEE, SQUIRREL EATS NUTS, SNAKE EATS THE SQUIRREL, GATOR EATS THE SNAKE. *And we can eat pretty much anything we want. It's the circle of life."*
>
> —Amy Burley

Ragin' Cajun Popcorn

1 TEASPOON SALT

¾ TEASPOON PAPRIKA

¾ TEASPOON SMOKED SWEET
PAPRIKA

½ TO ¾ TEASPOON CAYENNE
PEPPER

¾ TEASPOON LIGHT OR DARK
BROWN SUGAR

¼ TEASPOON FRESHLY
GROUND BLACK PEPPER

¼ TEASPOON ONION POWDER

¼ TEASPOON GARLIC POWDER

⅛ TEASPOON DRIED THYME,
CRUMBLED BETWEEN YOUR
FINGERTIPS

ABOUT 5 QUARTS UNSALTED,
UNBUTTERED, FRESHLY
POPPED POPCORN

3 TABLESPOONS UNSALTED
BUTTER, MELTED

In a small bowl, combine the salt, paprika, smoked sweet paprika, cayenne, brown sugar, pepper, onion powder, garlic powder, and thyme. Stir to combine, and break up any lumps with your fingers.

Put the popcorn in a giant bowl—one big enough so that you can toss the popcorn without sending kernels flying everywhere. Drizzle the butter over the popcorn while tossing with a large rubber spatula. Sprinkle with about one-half of the spice mixture, toss well, and then sprinkle with the rest. Toss vigorously, scraping along the bottom of the bowl where the unattached seasoning has collected, until the kernels are evenly coated. Serve right away.

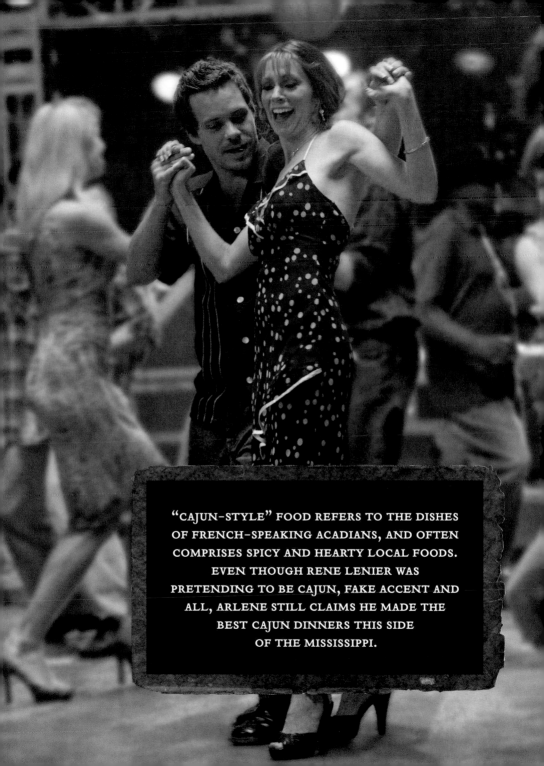

"CAJUN-STYLE" FOOD REFERS TO THE DISHES OF FRENCH-SPEAKING ACADIANS, AND OFTEN COMPRISES SPICY AND HEARTY LOCAL FOODS. EVEN THOUGH RENE LENIER WAS PRETENDING TO BE CAJUN, FAKE ACCENT AND ALL, ARLENE STILL CLAIMS HE MADE THE BEST CAJUN DINNERS THIS SIDE OF THE MISSISSIPPI.

One Crazy Cracker

ABOUT ½ CUP CHOPPED PECANS

4 OUNCES WHIPPED CREAM CHEESE

24 WATER CRACKERS

ABOUT ⅓ CUP RED PEPPER JELLY

FRESHLY GROUND BLACK PEPPER

MAKES 24 TOPPED CRACKERS, SERVES 6 TO 8

Toast the pecans in a small skillet over medium heat, stirring occasionally, until lightly browned and fragrant, 6 to 8 minutes. Transfer to a small bowl or plate and let cool.

Spread a generous 1 teaspoon cream cheese on each cracker, and then spoon a generous ½ teaspoon red pepper jelly onto the cream cheese. Sprinkle with black pepper and about 1 teaspoon or so of pecans. Serve.

"Sometimes I think that boy's cheese DONE SLID RIGHT OFF HIS CRACKER."

—Melinda Mickens

Cheese Spread for the Undead

1 GARLIC CLOVE, HALVED
LENGTHWISE

½ CUP MAYONNAISE, PLUS
MORE AS NEEDED

ONE 4-OUNCE JAR DICED
PIMIENTOS, DRAINED

1 TABLESPOON GRATED SWEET
ONION

¼ TEASPOON TABASCO SAUCE

DASH OF WORCESTERSHIRE
SAUCE

8 OUNCES YELLOW SHARP
CHEDDAR CHEESE, SHREDDED
(*Don't even think about using
the preshredded stuff!*)

CELERY STICKS AND/OR
CRACKERS FOR SERVING

**MAKES ABOUT 2 CUPS,
SERVES 6 TO 8**

Rub the inside of a medium mixing bowl with the cut sides of
the garlic clove. Press firmly to really work up the fragrance.
Discard the garlic or save it to annoy vamps.

Combine the mayonnaise, pimientos, grated onion, Tabasco,
and Worcestershire sauce in the bowl and stir to blend. Add
the cheese and mix well. If the mixture is too dry, stir in up
to 2 tablespoons more mayonnaise.

Transfer the cheese spread to a pretty bowl and serve to your
undead guests with celery sticks and/or crackers.

"I'D RATHER BE ALIVE

than undead."

—Sookie Stackhouse

Vamp Repellent

2 SMALLISH HEADS GARLIC

EXTRA-VIRGIN OLIVE OIL FOR DRIZZLING, PLUS 1 TABLESPOON

SALT AND FRESHLY GROUND BLACK PEPPER

ONE 15-OUNCE CAN CANNELLINI BEANS, RINSED AND DRAINED

ONE 8-OUNCE JAR ROASTED RED BELL PEPPERS, DRAINED AND PATTED DRY

3 TABLESPOONS GRATED PARMESAN CHEESE

2 TEASPOONS TOMATO PASTE

1½ TEASPOONS FRESH LEMON JUICE

¼ TEASPOON SMOKED SWEET PAPRIKA

PITA CHIPS, TOASTED BAGUETTE SLICES, AND/OR CRUDITÉS FOR SERVING

Preheat the oven to 350°F. Remove the papery outer skin from the garlic, leaving the heads intact, and then cut ¼ inch or so off the top of each one. Cut two sheets of aluminum foil and set a garlic head on each sheet, cut-side up. Lightly drizzle the garlic with olive oil and sprinkle with salt and pepper. Seal the edges of the foil and set the packets on a small baking sheet. Bake until the garlic is soft and creamy, about 45 minutes.

Carefully open the foil packets (watch out for steam!) and let the garlic cool for 15 minutes or so. Pull the cloves apart and remove the skins. Drop the pulp into a food processor. Add the 1 tablespoon olive oil, the beans, roasted peppers, Parmesan, tomato paste, lemon juice, and smoked paprika to the food processor and purée until the mixture is creamy and as smooth as it'll get, scraping down the bowl as needed. Season with salt and pepper. Transfer to a bowl, cover, and refrigerate to allow the flavors to meld, at least 2 hours.

Let the repellent stand at room temperature for about 30 minutes before serving with the dippers of choice.

MAKES ABOUT 2 CUPS, SERVES 6 TO 8

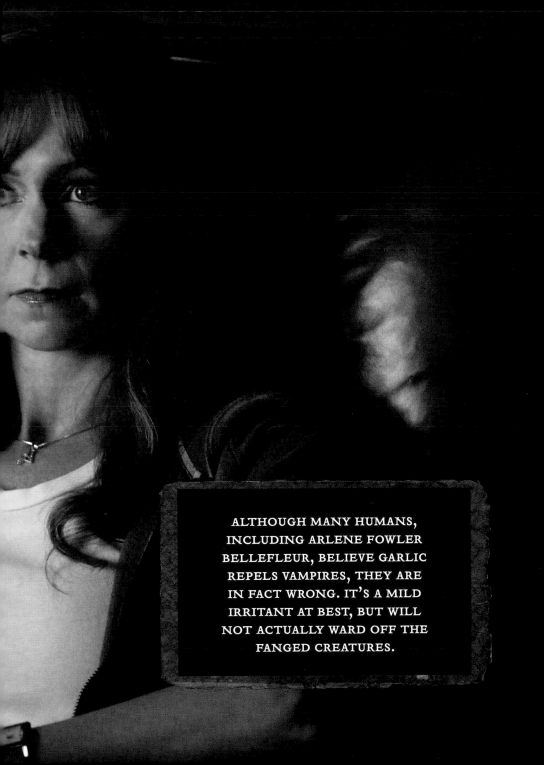

ALTHOUGH MANY HUMANS, INCLUDING ARLENE FOWLER BELLEFLEUR, BELIEVE GARLIC REPELS VAMPIRES, THEY ARE IN FACT WRONG. IT'S A MILD IRRITANT AT BEST, BUT WILL NOT ACTUALLY WARD OFF THE FANGED CREATURES.

Arti–Choked–to– Death Dip

ONE 14-OUNCE CAN ARTICHOKE HEARTS PACKED IN WATER, DRAINED

1 TABLESPOON UNSALTED BUTTER

½ SWEET ONION, FINELY CHOPPED

1 LARGE GARLIC CLOVE, MINCED

ONE 8-OUNCE PACKAGE CREAM CHEESE, AT ROOM TEMPERATURE

½ CUP MAYONNAISE

2 TABLESPOONS MINCED FRESH FLAT-LEAF PARSLEY

1 TABLESPOON FRESH LEMON JUICE

½ CUP GRATED PARMESAN CHEESE

SALT AND FRESHLY GROUND BLACK PEPPER

BAGUETTE SLICES, CRACKERS, OR PITA CHIPS FOR SERVING

"I tell you what, I am sick and tired of **WAITING AROUND TO GET STRANGLED."**

—Sookie Stackhouse

Position a rack in the upper third of the oven and preheat the oven to 400°F.

Gently squeeze each artichoke to remove excess water. Chop the artichokes and set them aside.

In an 8- or 9-inch cast-iron skillet (or other small skillet), melt the butter over medium heat. Add the onion and cook, stirring occasionally, until softened and translucent, about 5 minutes. Stir in the garlic and cook, stirring, until fragrant and no longer raw, about 1 minute. Transfer to a medium bowl and let cool slightly. If you've used a cast-iron skillet, you can use it to bake and serve the dip, so don't wash it out.

Add the cream cheese to the bowl with the onion and mix well with a rubber spatula, mashing the mixture to get it to combine. Add the mayonnaise, artichokes, parsley, lemon juice, and ⅓ cup of the Parmesan and stir until evenly distributed. Season with salt and pepper.

Put the dip back into the skillet if it's ovenproof, or into a shallow 1-quart baking dish, and spread it into an even layer. Sprinkle the remaining Parmesan evenly over the surface. Bake until the edges are gently bubbling and the dip is warmed throughout, 12 to 15 minutes. Turn on the broiler and broil until the surface is spotty brown, 2 to 3 minutes.

Let the dip cool for a few minutes, and then serve with the dippers of your choice.

Deviled Eggs of the Night

8 LARGE EGGS

⅓ CUP MAYONNAISE

2 OUNCES SMOKED HAM, MINCED

1 TABLESPOON CREOLE MUSTARD

SALT AND FRESHLY GROUND BLACK PEPPER

SRIRACHA SAUCE

MINCED FRESH CHIVES FOR GARNISH

MAKES 16 DEVILED-EGG HALVES, SERVES 8

"Steve Newlin's right! You're devils of the night!"

—protestors outside of Fangtasia

Put the eggs in a large saucepan and add enough water to cover them by about 1½ inches. Bring to a full boil over medium-high heat, cover the pan, turn off the heat, and set a timer for 10 minutes.

Meanwhile, fill a medium bowl with iced water. When the timer sounds, use a slotted spoon to transfer the eggs from the pan to the bowl. Let the eggs cool in the iced water for about 10 minutes.

Peel the eggs and cut each one in half lengthwise. Carefully remove the yolk from each half; set the whites aside. Grate the yolks on the small holes of a box grater into a medium bowl. Add the mayonnaise and mix well with a rubber spatula. Stir in the ham and mustard and season with salt and pepper, but be sure to taste the filling before seasoning because it may not need any salt at all.

Using two teaspoons, or a pastry bag fitted with a plain tip if you're feeling fancy, fill the egg-white halves with the yolk mixture. Top with Sriracha, sprinkle with chives, set on a platter, and serve.

Hot Date

16 LARGE, PLUMP DATES

ABOUT 2 OUNCES CREAM CHEESE

8 PICKLED JALAPEÑO SLICES, HALVED

8 SLICES BACON, HALVED CROSSWISE

Soak 16 wooden toothpicks in a bowl of warm water for about 30 minutes. Preheat the oven to 375°F. Line a rimmed baking sheet with aluminum foil or parchment paper (for easier cleanup) and set a wire rack on top.

Using a paring knife, make a slit along one side of each date (don't cut the dates in half by slicing all the way through). Remove the pits. Cut the cream cheese into ½-teaspoon-size pieces that will fit into the slit dates.

Fill each date with a piece or two of cream cheese—don't overstuff them—and then tuck in a pickled jalapeño half-slice. Pinch the date closed.

Lay a few of the bacon pieces on a work surface. Roll up a date, nice and snug, in each piece. Turn the date seam-side up if it isn't already, spear it through the side with a soaked toothpick, and set it on the wire rack. Repeat with the remaining bacon and dates.

Bake the bacon-wrapped dates until hot throughout and the bacon is browned and lightly crisped, about 25 minutes. Let cool for 5 minutes, and then transfer to a platter and serve right away.

"*You look like a porn star with that tan. And pink lipstick.* YOU GOT A DATE?"

—Lafayette Reynolds

Shrimp in a Pickle

6 CUPS WATER

3 OR 4 FRESH FLAT-LEAF PARSLEY SPRIGS

½ RED OR SWEET ONION; ¼ WITH ROOT END INTACT, ¼ VERY THINLY SLICED

5 GARLIC CLOVES; 2 CRUSHED, 3 THINLY SLICED

4 BAY LEAVES; 3 BROKEN IN HALF

½ TEASPOON CELERY SEEDS

½ TEASPOON BLACK PEPPERCORNS

1½ TEASPOONS SALT

1½ POUNDS LARGE SHRIMP (*26 to 30 per pound*), PEELED AND DEVEINED

4 STRIPS LEMON ZEST (*removed with a vegetable peeler*)

½ CUP EXTRA-VIRGIN OLIVE OIL

⅓ CUP FRESH LEMON JUICE

¼ CUP CIDER VINEGAR

½ TEASPOON FRESHLY GROUND BLACK PEPPER

½ TEASPOON YELLOW MUSTARD SEEDS

½ TEASPOON RED PEPPER FLAKES

SERVES 6 TO 8

CONTINUED

Pour the water into a medium saucepan and add the parsley, onion root end, crushed garlic, whole bay leaf, ¼ teaspoon of the celery seeds, peppercorns, and ½ teaspoon of the salt. Bring to a boil over medium-high heat, and then turn down the heat and simmer for 10 minutes to infuse the water with seasoning.

Raise the heat to high and bring the water back to a rolling boil. Add the shrimp, turn off the heat, cover the pan, and set a timer for 5 minutes.

Meanwhile, fill a medium bowl with ice water. When the timer sounds, the shrimp should be pink, firm, and opaque throughout (if they aren't, let them stand for another minute). Drain well, and then add the shrimp to the ice water to stop the cooking. Let stand for a few minutes until cool. Drain again and pick off any spices clinging to the shrimp.

In a clean 1½- to 2-quart glass jar, add the shrimp, sliced onion, sliced garlic, lemon zest, and broken bay leaves in alternating layers until all of it is in the jar. Whisk the olive oil, lemon juice, vinegar, remaining 1 teaspoon salt, pepper, mustard seeds, red pepper flakes, and remaining ¼ teaspoon celery seeds in a small nonreactive bowl, and then pour the mixture into the jar. The shrimp should be almost fully submerged. Cover the jar and let stand at room temperature for about 30 minutes.

Give the jar a good shake, and then refrigerate it for at least 8 hours or up to 3 days. Shake it from time to time to redistribute the contents.

Before serving, let the jar stand at room temperature for about 30 minutes. Skewer the shrimp on cocktail picks for serving or transfer the shrimp to a bowl and offer picks on the side.

A recipe for pickled shrimp has been in the Fortenberry family for several generations. When it got to Maxine, she decided to give it her own special touch: celery seed. SHE FIRST SERVED HER VERSION TO FRIENDS AND KIN WHO CAME TO HOYT'S FIFTH BIRTHDAY PARTY, AND IT WENT OVER SO WELL THAT SHE'S BEEN ADDING HER "SECRET" INGREDIENT EVER SINCE.

Killer Shrimp Cakes

Rémoulade

1 CUP MAYONNAISE

2 GREEN ONIONS (*white and green parts*), THINLY SLICED

2 TABLESPOONS KETCHUP

1½ TABLESPOONS CREOLE MUSTARD

1½ TEASPOONS PAPRIKA

1 TEASPOON TABASCO SAUCE

1 TEASPOON PREPARED HORSERADISH

¼ TEASPOON CELERY SALT

1 SMALL GARLIC CLOVE, MINCED TO A PASTE WITH A PINCH OF SALT

Shrimp Cakes

1 LARGE EGG

¼ CUP MAYONNAISE

½ TEASPOON SALT

¼ TEASPOON FRESHLY GROUND BLACK PEPPER

3 OR 4 DASHES TABASCO SAUCE

1 POUND SMALL OR MEDIUM SHRIMP, PEELED, DEVEINED, AND FINELY CHOPPED

2 GREEN ONIONS (*white and green parts*), THINLY SLICED

¼ CUP FINELY DICED RED BELL PEPPER

¾ CUP PLUS 2 TABLESPOONS PLAIN BREAD CRUMBS

⅓ CUP VEGETABLE OIL

When Sam Merlotte gets a new shipment of shrimp from the Gulf, he uses as much as he can for Lafayette's gumbo. But he always saves a little for a recipe closer to his heart: shrimp cakes. His adoptive mother, Sue Ann, would make them for him as a special treat.

To make the Rémoulade: Mix together all the ingredients in a small bowl. Cover and refrigerate.

To make the shrimp cakes: Line a baking sheet with parchment paper and set it aside. In a large bowl, beat the egg. Add the mayonnaise, salt, pepper, and Tabasco to the egg and mix well. Add the shrimp, green onions, and red bell pepper and mix until well combined. Sprinkle with ¼ cup plus 2 tablespoons of the bread crumbs and stir them in. The mixture will be thick and rather sticky.

Shape the mixture into two dozen little cakes, each one about a heaping 1 tablespoon in volume, about 1¾ inches in diameter, and just shy of ¾ inch thick. (You can moisten your hands with a little water if the mix-ture is super sticky.) Set the cakes on the prepared baking sheet. Cover and refrigerate for at least 30 minutes or up to 8 hours to firm up the cakes.

When you're ready to fry, put the remaining ½ cup bread crumbs in a wide, shallow bowl or baking dish. Line a baking sheet with a triple layer of paper towels and set a wire rack on top. Working with three or four at a time, coat the cakes on all sides with bread crumbs, pressing them in so the crumbs adhere. Return the cakes to the baking sheet.

In a heavy-bottomed 12-inch skillet, heat the vegetable oil over medium-high heat until shimmering. Add half of the cakes and cook, turning them once, until deeply browned on both sides, 5 to 6 minutes total. Transfer to the prepared wire rack and repeat with the remaining cakes.

Serve the shrimp cakes warm, with the rémoulade on the side for spoon-ing over or dipping into.

Cheese Stakes

◇◇

1 CUP UNBLEACHED ALL-PURPOSE FLOUR, PLUS
MORE FOR DUSTING

½ TEASPOON PAPRIKA

¼ TEASPOON CAYENNE PEPPER

½ TEASPOON SALT

6 TABLESPOONS COLD UNSALTED BUTTER, CUT
INTO ½-INCH CUBES

6 OUNCES SHARP YELLOW CHEDDAR CHEESE,
SHREDDED

2 TABLESPOONS WHOLE MILK OR HALF-AND-HALF

MAKES ABOUT
42 STAKES

◇◇

Position racks in the lower and upper thirds of the oven and preheat the
oven to 350°F. Line two large rimmed baking sheets with parchment
paper.

Combine the flour, paprika, cayenne, and salt in a food processor and
pulse to combine. Scatter the butter and cheese over the flour and
continue pulsing until the mixture resembles coarse crumbs, about
twenty quick pulses. Drizzle the milk over the flour-cheese mixture,
pulse a few times, and then let the machine run until a rough dough
ball forms, 15 to 20 seconds.

Transfer the dough to a lightly floured work surface, patting and squeez-
ing it to get it to really cohere. Divide the dough in half and set one piece
aside, covered with plastic wrap. Roll out the other piece to a rough
8-by-10-inch rectangle, about ⅛ inch thick, with a long edge near you.
Using a chef's knife, trim the edges to square them off (save the scraps),
and then cut the rectangle crosswise into elongated triangles, with the
wide end just shy of ¾ inch and the tapered end about ¼ inch wide. Cut,
alternating tip to tail; you should get about twenty stakes.

CONTINUED

Carefully transfer the stakes to the prepared baking sheet, spacing them about ½ inch apart. Toss any that break into the scrap pile. (If you have a special vamp to impress and you want to make your stakes a little fancy, gently twist each stake as you set it on the baking sheet and lightly press down on the twist to make it stay put.)

Repeat with the remaining dough half, and then gather up the scraps, roll them out, and cut a few more stakes.

Bake the stakes for about 16 minutes or until golden brown, rotating the baking sheets from top to bottom and front to back halfway through. (The points will brown more quickly than the wide ends.)

Let cool completely on the baking sheets. Carefully stand the stakes in a drinking glass or a wide cup and serve.

STAKES CAN BE MADE OUT OF ALMOST ANYTHING: PENCILS, CHAIR LEGS, EVEN A BROKEN TREE BRANCH. JUNIOR, PROPRIETOR OF THE ANTI-VAMPIRE SUPPLY STORE, THE STAKE HOUSE, USED TO ALWAYS SAY, "S'LONG AS IT'S WOOD, IT'S ALL GOOD."

Scorn Fritters

3 EARS FRESH CORN, SHUCKED

4 TO 5 CUPS VEGETABLE OIL FOR FRYING

¾ CUP UNBLEACHED ALL-PURPOSE FLOUR

¼ CUP PLUS 2 TABLESPOONS FINE STONE-GROUND YELLOW CORNMEAL

1½ TABLESPOONS SUGAR

¾ TEASPOON SALT

¼ TEASPOON CAYENNE PEPPER

1 LARGE EGG

⅔ CUP WHOLE MILK

1 TABLESPOON UNSALTED BUTTER, MELTED

MAPLE SYRUP OR CANE SYRUP FOR SERVING

Using a chef's knife, cut the kernels from the corn cobs and put in a medium bowl. After all the kernels have been cut off, run the back of the knife blade along the length of each cob to scrape out the milk. Discard the cobs and add the corn milk to the bowl with the kernels. You should have about 2½ cups of corn kernels and milk.

Line a rimmed baking sheet with a triple layer of paper towels, and set a wire rack on top. Pour the oil into a large, deep, heavy-bottomed saucepan to a depth of about 1½ inches. Set the pan over medium-high heat and heat the oil until it registers about 370°F on a deep-fry thermometer.

While the oil heats, in a large bowl, whisk together the flour, cornmeal, sugar, salt, and cayenne. In a medium bowl, whisk together the egg and whole milk until homogeneous. Pour the milk mixture into the flour mixture and whisk until the mixture is evenly moistened. Using a rubber spatula, fold in the butter, followed by the corn.

When the oil is hot enough, drop rounded tablespoons of batter into the hot oil; don't crowd the pan. Fry the fritters until rich golden brown on both sides, about 3 minutes, flipping them once or twice. Use a wire-mesh skimmer to lift out the fritters, letting the excess oil drain back into the pan, and set the fritters on the prepared wire rack. Fry the remaining batter in the same manner, but between batches, skim off any free-floating fritter bits in the oil and let the oil regain its heat.

Pile the fritters into a basket and serve with maple syrup. Or, if you want to rewarm them before serving, slide the baking sheet into a 250°F oven for 10 to 15 minutes.

"THIS S*** IS GOIN' FASTER
than fritters at a fat farm."

—Lafayette Reynolds

Mini–Mortal Spicy Corn and Cheddar Muffins

⅔ CUP UNBLEACHED ALL-PURPOSE FLOUR

½ CUP FINE STONE-GROUND YELLOW CORNMEAL

1 TABLESPOON SUGAR

1¼ TEASPOONS BAKING POWDER

¼ TEASPOON BAKING SODA

SCANT ½ TEASPOON SALT

⅔ CUP BUTTERMILK

1 LARGE EGG

2 TEASPOONS MINCED SEEDED CHIPOTLE CHILES IN ADOBO SAUCE

3 TABLESPOONS UNSALTED BUTTER, MELTED AND COOLED SLIGHTLY

2 OUNCES SHARP CHEDDAR CHEESE, SHREDDED

2 GREEN ONIONS (*white and green parts*), THINLY SLICED

Preheat the oven to 425°F. Grease a twenty-four-cup mini-muffin pan.

In a large bowl, whisk together the flour, cornmeal, sugar, baking powder, baking soda, and salt. In a small bowl, whisk together the buttermilk, egg, and chipotle chile until combined.

Pour the buttermilk mixture into the dry ingredients and whisk until almost combined. Add the butter and fold with a rubber spatula until the butter is incorporated. Add the cheese and green onions and fold in gently until evenly distributed. The batter will be thick.

Using two spoons, divide the batter evenly among the muffin cups; each one will be two-thirds to three-quarters full. Bake until the muffins are nicely risen and golden in color, 10 to 12 minutes.

Let the muffins cool in the pan for a few minutes, and then lift each one out onto a wire rack. Serve warm or at room temperature to both mini- and full-sized mortals. (To rewarm, set the muffins on a baking sheet and heat them in a 300°F oven for 5 to 7 minutes.)

"Now come on, Pam—they're funny. **THEY'RE LIKE HUMANS, BUT MINIATURE. TEACUP HUMANS."**

—Eric Northman

Werewolf Biscuits

6½ TABLESPOONS COLD UNSALTED BUTTER

1½ CUPS UNBLEACHED ALL-PURPOSE FLOUR,
PLUS MORE AS NEEDED

1¼ TEASPOONS BAKING POWDER

1 TEASPOON SUGAR

¼ TEASPOON SALT

⅛ TEASPOON BAKING SODA

¼ TEASPOON FRESHLY GROUND BLACK PEPPER

PINCH OF CAYENNE PEPPER

½ CUP VERY FINELY DICED RED BELL PEPPER

½ CUP PLUS 2 TABLESPOONS COLD BUTTERMILK

HONEY MUSTARD OR DIJON MUSTARD (*optional*)

ABOUT 6 OUNCES THINLY SLICED SMOKED HAM

ABOUT 4 OUNCES SHARP CHEDDAR CHEESE, THINLY SLICED

CONTINUED

Every werewolf pack has its own rules and rituals.
The Shreveport pack has a history of eating
its deceased packmasters.
They believe that taking in their packmaster's remains
will help keep his spirit alive for generations to come.

Preheat the oven to 475°F. Line a large baking sheet with parchment paper.

Cut up 5 tablespoons of the butter into ¼-inch cubes. Combine the flour, baking powder, sugar, salt, baking soda, black pepper, and cayenne in a food processor and pulse a few times to combine. Scatter the butter pieces over the flour mixture and pulse until just a few pieces of butter about the size of small peas remain. Transfer the flour mixture to a large bowl, add the red bell pepper, and toss with a rubber spatula until evenly distributed. Pour in the buttermilk and fold until the mixture forms a shaggy dough.

Transfer the dough onto a lightly floured work surface and knead gently just until it comes together. Gather the dough into a mound, flour the work surface once again, and then pat the mound into an even ½-inch thickness. Using a 1½-inch biscuit cutter dipped in flour, stamp out rounds of dough and set the rounds on the prepared baking sheet, turning them over so that the side that was against the work surface is now facing up, and spacing the rounds at least 1 inch apart. Gather, knead, and pat out the scraps, and then cut out additional rounds. You can repeat the process once more with the scraps, but the resulting biscuits will be a little less tender.

Melt the remaining 1½ tablespoons butter and brush on to the tops of the dough rounds. Slide the baking sheet into the oven. Immediately turn down the oven temperature to 450°F and bake until the biscuits are nicely risen and golden on the surface, 8 to 10 minutes. Let cool on the baking sheet.

When you're ready to serve, split the biscuits and spread mustard, if desired, on one or both cut sides. Lay slices of ham and cheese on the biscuit bottoms and set the tops in place. Arrange the biscuits on a platter and serve.

Skinwalkers

MAKES 24 MINI-STUFFED
POTATO HALVES

12 SMALL RED-SKINNED OR YUKON GOLD POTATOES, EACH ABOUT
1¼ INCHES IN DIAMETER

1 TABLESPOON EXTRA-VIRGIN OLIVE OIL

SALT AND FRESHLY GROUND BLACK PEPPER

3 SLICES BACON, CHOPPED FINE

3 TABLESPOONS SOUR CREAM

2 TABLESPOONS WHOLE MILK

2 GREEN ONIONS *(green part only)*, THINLY SLICED

½ CUP SHREDDED CHEDDAR CHEESE

TABASCO SAUCE

Place an oven rack in the middle of the oven and preheat the oven to 375°F.
Line a rimmed baking sheet with aluminum foil.

Cut each potato in half crosswise and put the halves in a bowl. Drizzle with
the olive oil, sprinkle with salt and pepper, and toss to coat. Place the potatoes
cut-side down on the prepared baking sheet and bake until the potatoes are
tender throughout, about 30 minutes.

Meanwhile, cook the bacon in a small skillet over medium-high heat, stirring
occasionally, until brown and crisp, about 7 minutes. Using a slotted spoon,
transfer the bacon to a paper towel–lined plate to drain.

Remove the potatoes from the oven and let cool for about 15 minutes. Use
a small serrated knife to trim the very tip of the rounded end of a potato
half so that it will sit stably. With a small melon baller or sharp-edged
½-teaspoon measuring spoon, scoop out the flesh, leaving a thin wall on
the sides and bottom. Drop the scooped guts into a medium bowl and return
the potato, hollowed-side up, to the baking sheet. Repeat with the remaining potato halves. You should have about 1 cup of potato flesh. Mash it with

a potato masher to break up large lumps, and then stir in the sour cream and milk until combined. Fold in the green onions, all but 3 tablespoons of the cheese, 2 dashes of Tabasco, and the bacon. Season with salt and pepper.

Preheat the broiler.

Using two spoons, stuff the potato halves with filling (about a scant 1 table-spoon in each half, depending on the size of the potato), mounding the filling. Sprinkle the reserved cheese on top of the stuffed potatoes. Broil the potatoes until the cheese on top is melted and browned, 3 to 4 minutes, rotating the baking sheet halfway through.

Let cool for a few minutes, and then transfer to a platter and serve.

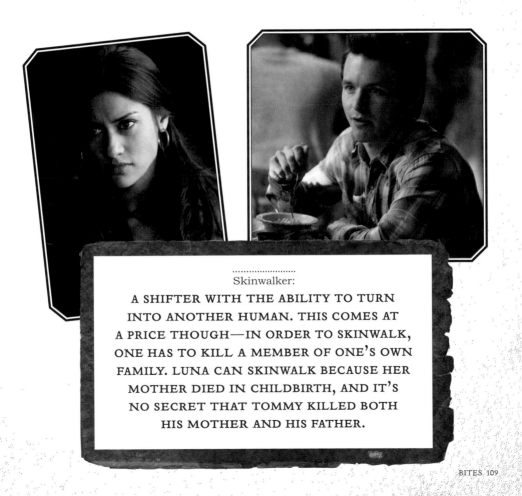

....
Skinwalker:

A SHIFTER WITH THE ABILITY TO TURN INTO ANOTHER HUMAN. THIS COMES AT A PRICE THOUGH—IN ORDER TO SKINWALK, ONE HAS TO KILL A MEMBER OF ONE'S OWN FAMILY. LUNA CAN SKINWALK BECAUSE HER MOTHER DIED IN CHILDBIRTH, AND IT'S NO SECRET THAT TOMMY KILLED BOTH HIS MOTHER AND HIS FATHER.

Friggin' Pigs in a Blanket

◇◇

1 SHEET FROZEN PUFF PASTRY FROM A 17.3-OUNCE BOX,
THAWED ACCORDING TO THE PACKAGE DIRECTIONS

1 LARGE EGG, BEATEN

6 LINKS ANDOUILLE SAUSAGE (*about 3 ounces each*)

¼ CUP PLUS 2 TABLESPOONS SESAME SEEDS

CREOLE MUSTARD FOR SERVING

◇◇

CONTINUED

**FORMER MERLOTTE'S WAITRESS
AND SAM'S EX-GIRLFRIEND**
*Daphne Landry was a shifter whose
go-to shift was, much to Andy
Bellefleur's dismay, a pig.*

On a lightly floured work surface, roll out the puff pastry to a 12-inch square; don't worry if the edges aren't perfectly straight. Using a pizza wheel or chef's knife, cut the square in half, and then cut each half crosswise into thirds so that you have six 4-by-6-inch rectangles.

Place a rectangle of dough so a short side is nearest you and brush the entire rectangle with beaten egg, especially the edge farthest away. Set an andouille link on top just inside the edge nearest you and roll up the sausage tightly in the dough; it's fine if the ends poke out a bit. Pinch the seam to seal and set the dough-wrapped sausage on a tray or baking sheet. Repeat with the remaining rectangles of dough and sausages, cover with plastic wrap, and refrigerate for about 1 hour to firm up the dough. Save the remaining egg.

Preheat the oven to 400°F. Line two rimmed baking sheets with parchment paper. Spread out the sesame seeds on a plate.

Working one at a time, brush the dough-wrapped sausages with the remaining egg and roll in the sesame seeds, sprinkling more on as needed, until evenly coated. Using a serrated knife, trim the protruding ends of the sausage, and then cut the sausage evenly into five pieces; each will be about ¾ inch. Don't worry if the blankie is a little loose around the piggy. Set the pieces cut-side up on a prepared baking sheet. Repeat with the remaining sausages and sesame seeds, and place fifteen piggies in blankies on each baking sheet.

Bake the piggies, one baking sheet at a time, for 15 minutes, and then use a wide spatula to flip each piece. Continue to bake until nicely browned, about 5 minutes longer. Serve warm or at room temperature with Creole mustard. (To rewarm the friggin' piggies, put them in a 350°F oven for about 5 minutes.)

Terry B's Mini-Burgers

8 SLICES BACON

1 TABLESPOON VEGETABLE OIL

1 EXTRA-LARGE OR 2 SMALL SWEET ONIONS, THINLY SLICED

SALT AND FRESHLY GROUND BLACK PEPPER

¼ TEASPOON CHILI POWDER

1½ POUNDS GROUND BEEF

8 MINI-BUNS, ABOUT 3 INCHES IN DIAMETER, SPLIT

ABOUT 4 OUNCES CHEDDAR CHEESE, THINLY SLICED

PICKLED OKRA OR JALAPEÑO SLICES (*optional*)

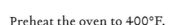

Preheat the oven to 400°F.

Lay the bacon slices in a single layer on a rimmed baking sheet. Bake until the bacon is browned and crisp, 12 to 15 minutes, rotating the baking sheet halfway through. Transfer the bacon to a paper towel–lined plate and pour the bacon grease into a small bowl. Set both aside. Resist eating the bacon!

While the bacon cooks, heat the vegetable oil in a 12-inch skillet over high heat. Add the onions and ½ teaspoon salt and stir until coated with fat. Cook, stirring frequently, until the onions just begin to color, about 3 minutes. Turn down the heat to medium-high and continue to cook, stirring occasionally, until the onions are medium golden brown and softened, but retain a bit of crunch, about 10 minutes. Season with pepper and set the onions aside.

CONTINUED

In a small bowl or ramekin, stir together the chili powder and ¼ teaspoon salt. In a large bowl, break apart the ground beef and sprinkle with ¾ teaspoon salt and ½ teaspoon pepper. Drizzle 1½ tablespoons of the reserved bacon grease over the beef, and gently work it in, along with the salt and pepper—don't compact the meat or the burgers will be dense and tough. Shape the beef into eight evenly sized patties, each weighing 3 ounces, and just a little larger than the buns. Press a little indentation into the center of each patty so they won't bloat up when you cook them. Season on both sides with the chili powder mixture. Brush the cut sides of the buns lightly with some of the remaining bacon grease.

Build a hot fire in a charcoal grill or turn the burners of a gas grill to high. Let the cooking grate heat for a few minutes, and then scrape it clean.

Grill the patties, flipping them once, until nicely browned on both sides, about 5 minutes total for medium (or about 7 minutes if you want them well-done). Toast the cut sides of the buns on the grill until lightly grill-marked, about 15 seconds.

Set a patty on the bottom of each bun and top with cheese, bacon (break each slice in half first), sautéed onion, pickled okra (if desired), and, finally, the top of the bun. Serve right away.

Everyone at Merlotte's has his strong suit:
Sam's succotash is the best in three
parishes, Lafayette's in charge of the
gumbo, and Terry's known for making
the tastiest burgers in town, whether it's
at Merlotte's or in his own backyard.

Stackhouse Ribs

Ribs

1 TABLESPOON PAPRIKA

1 TABLESPOON LIGHT BROWN SUGAR

1½ TEASPOONS CHILI POWDER

1½ TEASPOONS GARLIC POWDER

1¼ TEASPOONS SALT

1 TEASPOON FRESHLY GROUND
BLACK PEPPER

¾ TEASPOON GROUND CUMIN

½ TEASPOON ONION POWDER

½ TEASPOON POWDERED MUSTARD

¼ TEASPOON CAYENNE

2 RACKS PORK BABY BACK RIBS
(about 2¼ pounds each)

Sauce

TWO 12-OUNCE CANS ROOT BEER
(Don't use diet!)

¾ CUP KETCHUP

¾ CUP PACKED LIGHT BROWN SUGAR

¼ CUP PLUS 2 TABLESPOONS CIDER
VINEGAR

2 TABLESPOONS CREOLE MUSTARD

¾ TEASPOON RED PEPPER FLAKES

¾ TEASPOON SALT

*"Without
that sanctimonious
little prick Godric
to save you,* I would
just love to rip
you open and wear
your ribcage
as a hat."

—Lorena Krasiki

To make the ribs: Combine the spices and seasonings in small bowl and mix well with your fingers. Sprinkle the rib racks with the spice rub, focusing on the meaty sides, but make sure all surfaces are seasoned. Pat the spice rub to get it to stick, but don't rub it into the meat, because your fingers will get all gummed up. Wrap the ribs in plastic wrap and refrigerate for at least 4 hours or up to 2 days.

When you're ready to cook the ribs, unwrap them, set the racks meat-side up on a rimmed baking sheet, and let them stand at room temperature for about 30 minutes. Preheat the oven to 325°F.

Cover the ribs and baking sheet tightly with a sheet of extra-wide aluminum foil. Bake for 45 minutes, and then remove the foil. Continue to bake the ribs until a skewer inserted into the meaty parts between the bones meets very little resistance, about 45 minutes longer. Let the ribs rest on the baking sheet. (The ribs can be cooked to this point, cooled, and held at room temperature for 1 or 2 hours. Or, you can wrap the cooled ribs in foil and refrigerate them overnight; let them stand at room temperature for about 1 hour before proceeding.)

To make the sauce: Combine all the ingredients in a large nonreactive saucepan and whisk well. Bring to a boil over high heat, and then turn down the heat to maintain a lively simmer. Cook, stirring occasionally, until the sauce is dark, glossy, thickened, and reduced to just shy of 2 cups, about 30 minutes. Measure about ¾ cup into a bowl for passing at the table.

Build a medium-low fire in a charcoal grill or turn the burners of a gas grill to medium-low heat. Let the cooking grate heat for a few minutes, and then scrape it clean.

Brush the ribs all over with sauce and set them on the grill. Cook, turning the racks every 3 to 5 minutes and brushing them with additional sauce, until they're heated through and nicely glazed, with some charred spots, 15 to 20 minutes. Transfer the racks to a cutting board and give them a final brushing of sauce.

Using a chef's knife, cut between the bones to divide the racks into individual ribs. Pile the ribs onto a platter and serve with the reserved sauce and a mountain of napkins.

Dead Red Cupcakes

MAKES 12 CUPCAKES

Cupcakes

1¼ CUPS CAKE FLOUR

1½ TABLESPOONS UNSWEETENED COCOA POWDER

½ TEASPOON BAKING SODA

1 TABLESPOON RED FOOD COLORING

1¼ TEASPOONS DISTILLED WHITE VINEGAR

¾ TEASPOON VANILLA EXTRACT

½ CUP BUTTERMILK

5 TABLESPOONS UNSALTED BUTTER, AT ROOM TEMPERATURE

¾ CUP GRANULATED SUGAR

½ TEASPOON SALT

1 LARGE EGG, AT ROOM TEMPERATURE

Frosting

ONE 8-OUNCE PACKAGE CREAM CHEESE, AT ROOM TEMPERATURE

½ CUP (*1 stick*) UNSALTED BUTTER, AT ROOM TEMPERATURE

1 TEASPOON VANILLA EXTRACT

2 CUPS CONFECTIONERS' SUGAR

Red Drizzle

⅓ CUP SEEDLESS RASPBERRY JAM

1 TABLESPOON POMEGRANATE, CRANBERRY, OR CHERRY JUICE, PLUS MORE AS NEEDED

12 FRESH RASPBERRIES

CONTINUED

> "*Dear Hoyt,*
> *You are my first and*
> *only born, and if you think I am going*
> *to sit back and watch you throw your*
> *life away on a redheaded dead girl,*
> *you are sorely mistaken.*
> **THERE WILL BE CONSEQUENCES.**"
>
> —— Maxine Fortenberry

To make the cupcakes: Preheat the oven to 350°F. Line a standard twelve-cup muffin pan with baking cups.

Sift the flour, cocoa powder, and baking soda into a medium bowl. Stir the food coloring, vinegar, and vanilla into the buttermilk until the mixture is uniformly shocking in color.

Using an electric mixer at medium-high speed, beat the butter, granulated sugar, and salt in a large bowl until light and aerated, about 3 minutes. Scrape down the bowl with a rubber spatula, add the egg, and beat until well combined, about 1 minute. Scrape down the bowl once again. With the mixer running on low speed, add the flour mixture in three batches, alternately with the buttermilk in two batches, mixing until just combined after each addition. Give the batter a few gentle folds with the rubber spatula, scraping along the bottom and sides of the bowl to make sure that the color is homogeneous.

Using a spring-loaded ice-cream scoop or two soupspoons, divide the batter evenly among the muffin cups; each cup should be roughly two-thirds full. Bake until well risen and a toothpick inserted into one of the centermost cupcakes comes out clean, about 20 minutes. Let the cupcakes cool in the pan on a wire rack for 10 minutes, and then carefully lift each one out of the pan and onto the rack. Let cool to room temperature.

To make the frosting: With an electric mixer at medium-high speed, beat the cream cheese and butter in a large bowl until well combined and fully softened, about 3 minutes. Scrape down the bowl, and beat in the vanilla. Reduce the mixer speed to low, and gradually add the confectioners' sugar. When all the sugar is in, increase the speed to medium-high and beat until the frosting is light and fluffy, about 1 minute. Give the frosting a few stirs. If it's extremely soft, chill it for a few minutes in the refrigerator.

Fit a large pastry bag with a plain tip about ½ inch in diameter and fill the bag with the frosting. If you don't own a pastry bag, you'll need to work in two batches. Put about one-half of the frosting into a large zipper-lock bag, push the frosting to one corner, and snip off the tip of the bag so that there's an opening of about ½ inch. Pipe the frosting onto each cupcake in a spiral, starting at the edge and ending in the center. If piping isn't your thing, just spread the frosting onto each cupcake, trying to create a nice mound. Set the frosted cupcakes aside.

To make the red drizzle: In a small bowl, whisk together the raspberry jam and pomegranate juice until smooth. The mixture should be thick, but pourable. Spoon ½ teaspoon or so onto the surface of an uncut orange or lemon—it should flow down the sides of the fruit very slowly. If the drizzle is too thick, whisk in additional juice, ½ teaspoon at a time, until the consistency is just right.

Spoon about ½ teaspoon of red drizzle onto the center of each cupcake, letting the drizzle flow down as it may. Create additional drops and drips as desired. Once all the cupcakes are good and drizzled, press a raspberry into the peak of each cupcake and dab a bit more jam mixture on top of each berry. Serve within 1 hour or so, or refrigerate, uncovered, for up to 12 hours (if chilled, let the cupcakes stand at room temperature for about 30 minutes before serving).

Pecan Pie Bars of Wisdom

Crust

7 TABLESPOONS UNSALTED BUTTER, AT ROOM TEMPERATURE

1/3 CUP GRANULATED SUGAR

3/4 TEASPOON SALT

1/2 TEASPOON VANILLA EXTRACT

1 1/4 CUPS UNBLEACHED ALL-PURPOSE FLOUR

Filling

1 1/2 CUPS PECANS, COARSELY CHOPPED

5 TABLESPOONS UNSALTED BUTTER

2/3 CUP PACKED DARK BROWN SUGAR

1/2 TEASPOON SALT

1/4 CUP PLUS 2 TABLESPOONS LIGHT CORN SYRUP

2 LARGE EGGS, BEATEN

2 TEASPOONS VANILLA EXTRACT

To make the crust: Preheat the oven to 350°F. Cut two sheets of aluminum foil, each about 15 inches long, and fold lengthwise to 8-inch widths. Line the bottom of a 9-inch square pan with the foil sheets, one on top of the other, so they are perpendicular to each other, pressing the foil into the corners and up the sides of the pan. There should be a few of inches of overhang, which will help you remove the bars later on. Coat the foil with nonstick cooking spray.

Using an electric mixer at medium-high speed, beat the butter, granulated sugar, and salt in a medium bowl until light and aerated, about 3 minutes. Scrape down the bowl with a rubber spatula, add the vanilla, and beat at medium-high until well combined, about 1 minute. Scrape down the bowl once again. Reduce the mixer speed to low, gradually add the flour, and mix for about 20 seconds. Scrape down the bottom and sides of the bowl and continue to mix on low speed until the mixture is crumby and evenly moistened, about 30 seconds longer.

Empty the crust mixture into the prepared baking pan. Using your hands, press the crumbs firmly into an even layer. Bake until golden (the edges will be a couple of shades darker than the rest), 20 to 22 minutes.

While the crust is baking, prepare the filling: Toast the pecans in a medium skillet over medium heat, stirring occasionally, until lightly browned and fragrant, 8 to 10 minutes. Transfer the nuts to a small bowl or plate and let cool. In a medium saucepan over medium heat, melt the butter with the brown sugar and salt, whisking to combine and breaking up any sugar lumps. When the butter has melted and the sugar has dissolved, remove the pan from the heat and whisk in the corn syrup. Let cool until barely warm to the touch, and then whisk in the eggs and vanilla until the filling is homogeneous. Set aside until needed.

Immediately after removing the crust from the oven, add the pecans to the filling mixture in the saucepan and stir to combine. Pour the filling over the hot crust and return the baking pan to the oven. (If your crust has been out of the oven for a while and is no longer hot, warm it up in the oven for about 5 minutes before pouring in the filling.) Reduce the oven temperature to 325°F and bake until the filling is set and beginning to form one or two small cracks on the surface, about 25 minutes.

Let cool completely in the pan on a wire rack, about 1½ hours. Using the foil overhang, carefully lift the square out of the pan. Using a chef's knife coated with nonstick cooking spray, cut the square into twenty evenly sized rectangles. Serve immediately or store in an airtight container for a few days (the crust will soften a bit, but the flavor won't suffer).

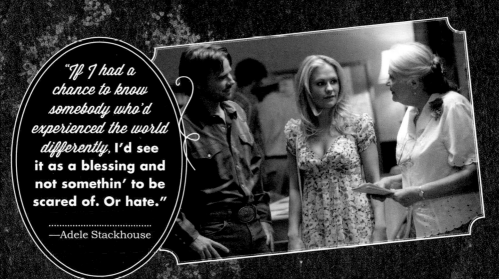

"If I had a chance to know somebody who'd experienced the world differently, I'd see it as a blessing and not somethin' to be scared of. Or hate."

—Adele Stackhouse

INDEX

TABLE OF EQUIVALENTS

The exact equivalents in the following
tables have been rounded for convenience.

Liquid/Dry Measurements

U.S.	Metric
¼ TEASPOON	1.25 MILLILITERS
½ TEASPOON	2.5 MILLILITERS
1 TEASPOON	5 MILLILITERS
1 TABLESPOON (3 TEASPOONS)	15 MILLILITERS
1 FLUID OUNCE (2 TABLESPOONS)	30 MILLILITERS
¼ CUP	60 MILLILITERS
⅓ CUP	80 MILLILITERS
½ CUP	120 MILLILITERS
1 CUP	240 MILLILITERS
1 PINT (2 CUPS)	480 MILLILITERS
1 QUART (4 CUPS, 32 OUNCES)	960 MILLILITERS
1 GALLON (4 QUARTS)	3.8 LITERS
1 OUNCE (BY WEIGHT)	30 GRAMS
1 POUND	450 GRAMS
2.2 POUNDS	1 KILOGRAM

Lengths

U.S.	Metric
⅛ INCH	3 MILLIMETERS
¼ INCH	6 MILLIMETERS
½ INCH	12 MILLIMETERS
1 INCH	2.5 CENTIMETERS

OVEN TEMPERATURE

Fahrenheit	Celsius	Gas
250	120	½
275	140	1
300	150	2
325	160	3
350	180	4
375	190	5
400	200	6
425	220	7
450	230	8
475	240	9
500	260	10